GROWING

—— UP ——

RED BANK

LISA NOEL

WRITERS REPUBLIC L.L.C.
515 Summit Ave. Unit R1
Union City, NJ 07087, USA

Website: *www.writersrepublic.com*
Hotline: *1-877-656-6838*
Email: *info@writersrepublic.com*

Ordering Information:
Quantity sales. Special discounts are available on quantity purchases by corporations, associations, and others. For details, contact the publisher at the address above.

Library of Congress Control Number: 2020931786
ISBN-13:   978-1-64620-127-3   [Paperback Edition]
                  978-1-64620-261-4   [Digital Edition]

Rev. date: 03/17/2020

CONTENTS

I am dedicating this book to my family, my friends, and my hometown of Red Bank for being the contributors and inspiration for all of my stories.

And to my grandson Keaston. Who will grow up with his own stories to tell.

DINNER
FOR MOM AND DAD

This story is dedicated to my older brother Anthony.
This was your idea.

I will forever be traumatized because of my older brother Anthony.

Every year Anthony and I would always put some of our allowance money together to buy our parents something for the Holidays, their Birthdays, Anniversary's, whatever.

So, when Anthony asked me what I think we should do this year, I couldn't think of anything. At least nothing we could agree on. So I said we should ask grandma.

This grandma is our fathers mother "Nora". She lived with us and she suggested we should do something different. Something we haven't done before, Like cook dinner for them.

Now with Anthony being the oldest, he should of known damn well that the two of us cooking dinner was not a good idea. But nooo Anthony went and said "Oh yeah! We can do that!" I should have said something. But I didn't. I just stood there and went along with it like a fool.

Then grandma topped it off when she said "Y'all better get something easy that you know you can cook. Because I'm not gonna help you."

Now that should've been our cue to back out of this and think of something else, right? Anyone in their right mind would've. But not Anthony. He told grandma, "That's okay grandma. We won't need your help. We can do this.

So that night Anthony came into my room and told me he has decided on what we are gonna cook. He has decided. He didn't ask me my opinion at all. And yet, he wanted my money to get the food. All of it.

Now, when Anthony said he needed all of my money, I really had to think twice about that. Because at that time I was getting three dollars a week for my allowance. Not to mention the extra I was able to con out of my father. Besides, a girl has needs, you know, and those needs weren't cheap. A Coffee Cake, something I love, cost thirty cents, an Icee cost a quarter, a big pack or Banana Now & Laters cost twenty cents each, and a pack of Bubblicous Bubble Gum cost ten cents a pack, and a Blow Pop cost a nickel each. This was my shopping list every week. So giving up my three dollars wasn't easy for me. Thank God I had stuff stashed away for a rainy day or Anthony never would have got my three dollars.

At the time I didn't know Anthony was getting ten dollars a week for his allowance. Because if I had, there would've been problems, okay? That's just not fair. You don't do that, you know. Besides I felt like I earned every dime of my three-dollar allowance. I had to deal with three boys and survive, and all Anthony had to do was take out the garbage.

So the next day Anthony went shopping and came home with the food we were supposed to cook that night. He hid it upstairs in his room until our parents left for their date that night. Since they were going out, and it was a weekend, they ordered us pizza for dinner that night.

After we ate, my little brothers, Lee and Keith, and I took our baths and got ready for bed. Lee and Keith had to go straight to bed. I could stay up until they got back as long as I had my pajamas on. Anthony was allowed to take his bath and go to bed whenever he wanted to on the weekends. Which I also didn't think was fair, but

I didn't bring it up that night because we just wanted our parents to hurry up and leave the house.

So as soon as their car left the driveway, Anthony ran upstairs to get the food he bought. He came downstairs with a bag of white potatoes (But that was okay. We could bake those.), a bag of collard greens, some fat meat, some beer, and ten live crabs. I couldn't believe it. To do what? I knew nothing about no collard greens, fat meat, or live crabs. And the beer, what was that for? Come on now! Remember, I was only eight.

I looked at Anthony and said, "You have got to be crazy. I don't know how to cook this stuff! Why did you buy this? Grandma already said to buy stuff we could cook because she wasn't gonna help us. I thought you were gonna buy some hot dogs or something, not no collard greens and crabs…I want my money back."

While we were arguing, Anthony said, "Oh, stop complaining. We can do this. I know we can. My friend Kent went shopping with me, and told me what to do."

I said, "Kent? Kent? Really? You're listening to Kent now?"

Because I knew who he was talking about. Kent was my brother's best friend and road dog, and I didn't consider either of them very smart. I mean, they're boys.

Anthony said Yes. And all I had to do was shut up, listen to him and do what he told me.

Why did I ever believe him? I don't know.

But the first thing he told me to do was to rinse off the potatoes and pass them to him, which I did. Then he wrapped them in aluminum foil and put them in the oven. That went well with no problems. Then he told me to wash the collard greens and to wash them good because sometimes they had bugs on them. As he filled a pot with water, dropped in the fat meat and waited for it to boil.

But I didn't know how to wash no collard greens. So I just dumped them in the sink and filled the sink with hot water, Dove dishwashing liquid, and some bleach. And I washed them collards until they squeaked. You would think Anthony would've stopped me, right? But he didn't. So while I was doing that, Anthony filled another pot with the beer he bought and put it on the stove. I was wondering what the beer was for. I mean who Boil's crab's in beer? But I didn't say anything.

After I finished, I pulled the chair I was using to stand on (remember, I was only eight) while I was washing the collards over to the stove and stuffed those collards in that boiling pot of greasy fat-meat water.

We thought everything was going good, right? And it was until the beer started boiling and it was time for Anthony to get the crabs and put them in the pot. The first two crabs went in okay. But after that all hell broke loose and it became a fight for survival. Anthony tried to put the other crabs in the pot, and just as fast as he put one in the pot and lifted the pot lid for the others, those crabs would pop out. Every time he lifted the lid another crab would pop back out. And before Anthony could figure out what to do, we had seven crabs running for their lives all over the kitchen floor, snapping at our feet and fighting each other.

Anthony started yelling at me to help him catch the crabs, and I did. Or at least I tried. Until one of those crabs clamped down on my toe. Now I have been in pain before. But not like that. That little sucker just would not let go. I swear, I think he was trying to take my toe off. After that I was done. I started jumping around, screaming, while trying to get that crab off my toe with no help from my big brother Anthony. He was too busy yelling at me to stop jumping around before I step on them.

Grandma was sitting on the couch near the kitchen doorway laughing at us so hard she starting choking on her snuff.

For those of you who don't know what snuff is. It's tobacco that has been grounded into fine powder. People put it in their mouth, between their lip and their teeth. And it comes in a small tin can. Nasty stuff. Never try it.

But anyway, with Grandma laughing, Anthony yelling at me, and me screaming and jumping around, my dog, Butch, came running from upstairs (where he wasn't supposed to be in the first place) to protect me, growling and snarling. Butch pulled that crab off my toe, shook it, and slammed it down on the kitchen floor. Then jumped on the others and slung them around until they fell apart.

I ran over to Grandma, who was still laughing, and jumped on the couch with her.

After Butch was done killing all the crabs, he sat down and started making a meal out of a few of the bodies. Anthony was so mad he couldn't say or do nothing but pick up the crab legs that were scattered all over the floor before Butch went for those too.

While all this was happening and I was still on the couch with grandma crying about my toe, the collard greens started boiling and soap bubbles started coming out of the pot and was running all over the stove, oven, and floor. This is why Anthony shouldn't have told an eight-year-old to wash collard greens. But, of course, Anthony blamed me for everything. While calling me stupid for the bubbly collards, he told me to shut up and stop whining about my toe and to get up and help him clean up the mess!

Now, I heard Anthony loud and clear when he called me stupid, but I chose not to respond at that time because I was still traumatized by those crabs from hell. Besides Grandma was still laughing at us, even with me sitting right there on the couch with her. So I did. I got up to help him because I just wanted to hurry up and get that dinner over and done with.

Now, even though I was already helping him, he continued yelling at me. I turned off the stove to stop the soap bubbles while he cleaned up what Butch left. He washed off the crab legs that Butch didn't chew up and put them back in the pot with the crabs that didn't escape, which was only the first two or three. Then he started yelling at me again.

"Get the pot of collard greens, and drain the water out into the sink, stupid."

Stupid? Really? He called me stupid again? So now I was mad. He thinks he's gonna keep yelling orders at me and calling me stupid when I'm here helping him clean up this mess he made. This was all his fault anyway because if he hadn't bought those damn crabs none of this would've happened.

So I told him, "No! I'm not helping you do nothing else. I'm done. Because for one, I can't reach that pot without standing on a chair. For two, I can't lift that pot. It's full of water and collards. It's too heavy. And for three, because you keep yelling at me and calling me stupid. So no! I'm not doing anything else for you. Since I'm so stupid, you do it yourself."

Then when I turned around to walk away, Anthony pushed me in my back and told me to get out of the kitchen and called me a big baby.

A big baby? After all the work I did? Oh, that really pissed me off. So I turned around and pushed him back. Then he popped me upside my head. And it was on! We started fighting.

Well, I was doing all the fighting, because every time me and Anthony got in a fight, I'm the one that got all tired and worn out. Because Anthony would just put his hand on my forehead and push me back, holding me like that. And I would be screaming, punching, kicking, and swinging at nothing. He knew I was too small for any of my kicks and punches to reach him or hurt him.

And while Anthony and I were doing all this fighting and arguing, the potatoes were still in the oven, burning.

That was when Grandma yelled for us to stop it. "Stop all that fighting and arguing! Now, either finish cooking the food or throw it away because you're burning up the potatoes!"

So, after Anthony let go of my forehead, I kicked him in his leg, ran behind Grandma, and told her I wasn't doing nothing else, that Anthony should have just got some hot dogs and chips or something instead of spending all of my money on those crazy crabs.

Grandma said, "Okay, okay. Forget it. Get over here, sit down, and keep your mouth shut. Anthony, drain the water out of those collards, leave everything the way it is, and get ready for bed. It's over."

While Anthony drained the collards, turned off the crabs, and went to take a shower, I lay down on the couch with my head on Grandma's lap and watched TV. But I was still mad. (Hell, I'm a Taurus and we hold grudges, you know?). And I had a plan. I was just waiting for our parents to come home because I was going to make sure Anthony got a whooping. Even though he hardly ever got whoopings, I was going to make sure he got one tonight. My plan was to tell them that Anthony bought beer that he said was for the crabs but he drank some of it before he put it in the pot. Even though I knew it was a lie, I didn't care. He called me stupid, pushed me, and hit me upside my head. I had to get my revenge somehow. I was going to make sure I have tears in my eyes and everything. Oh, I was ready. My plan was set.

Even though we were always fighting about something, because I was born with Sickle Cell Disease and was always in the hospital hitting me was a big No-No. So I had my story in my head and my tears all ready to go. I was just waiting for our parents to walk through that back door. But I ended up falling asleep. (See what happens when you plan to do dirty.)

I found out the next morning that when Anthony came out of the bathroom after taking his shower, Grandma told him he could go to bed too. So he carried me upstairs with him and put me in my bed like he always did when I was sick or fell asleep downstairs and then went to his room.

Even though Grandma said she wasn't going to help us, she did. She took over. She threw out the burned potatoes and made some more, threw out the collards, popped a can of biscuits, put them in the oven and asved what was left of the crabs then set the table for two with a new table cloth and the good dishes, glasses, and silverware from the china cabinet. And our parents loved it.

But Grandma didn't have a chance to tell us about it because as soon as me and Anthony got up that morning and went downstairs, our mother and father thanked us for the dinner we made for them. They said Grandma told them how me and Anthony did everything all by ourselves with no help from her and that the food was really good and how they were so proud of us because she said we did it all without fighting.

They were so happy. And even though I was still mad with Anthony, hearing how proud they were just blew my plan out of my head. I didn't want them to think my grandma was a liar, and I didn't want them to be disappointed in me or Anthony.

In the end Grandma really did come through. And I don't mess with crabs to this day.

The End.

LEE

This story is dedicated to my oldest little brother who couldn't keep a secret to save his life.

Okay, several years after leaving my grandma and uncle's house, my mother and father had two more boys. Like I didn't have enough problems on my hands dealing with my older brother, Anthony.

Lee, the oldest of the two and six years younger than me, thought everything belonged to him. And if he got his hands on my stuff, he would break it. So I had to make sure my stuff was hidden from him or at least far enough up so he couldn't reach it.

But one thing we noticed about him after he learned to talk is that Lee could never keep a secret. It didn't matter what is was, if you said anything around him, he would repeat it to anybody who would listen.

One year my mom decided she wanted a new makeover for the living room of our house. She didn't want to change the floor plan or anything, she just wanted some new wallpaper and carpeting.

So my father hired a friend of his, whose name was Mr. Buck, for the job. Now Mr. Buck was the one my father always called whenever there was work to be done around the house. Mr. Buck was quick and reliable. Oh, he could do little stuff like fix the toilet or a messed-up light, but when it came to a job like this, I didn't think he could do it, especially since he always worked alone.

But even though Mr. Buck was a very nice man, he was one of those men that never wore a coat in the winter. (This is in New Jersey.)

And since he always wore a tool belt around his waist, everyone could always see the crack of his butt. Well, not the crack of his butt, you could see his whole ass, okay? The whole thing. At all times. Even when he wasn't bending down.

He is the kind of person who always showed up to do the job at dinnertime and was always hungry. And if you offered to let him eat with you, he wouldn't get up from the table until all the meat was gone. Even if you told him the rest of the family isn't home yet and hasn't eaten, he would say things like, "Ummp, this is so good. I'm gonna get me just a little bit more" or "If you don't mind, I'm gonna get just one more bite," until every bite of meat is gone. The kind of person who would pick his nose, pick his teeth, and burp at the table…just nasty!

And my mom and grandma hated him. Maybe I shouldn't say hate. I'll just say they did not like this man with a passion. Because, not only did you have to look at his butt all day and he didn't have any manners at the dinner table, he was also really messy with his work. He never cleaned up after himself. He would just drop his stuff on the floor and just leave it there for us to clean up. And he stank.

I mean, this man didn't just stink like a hardworking-man-coming- home-to-take-a-shower stink. No. He stank like he never had a bath in his life, sweat like a pig no matter how cold it was, and wore the same dirty unwashed clothes every day. Don't touch him because he most definitely has the cooties. OMG, you can still smell him in the house days after he's gone. That kind of stank.

And as soon as he walked in the house my grandma would try to find an excuse to leave just to escape the smell of Mr. Buck by saying, "Well, I think I'm gonna go over Shel's (her daughter) house. I'll be back tomorrow." And my mom would say, "Oh no, you're not leaving me here alone. If I have to stay here and smell him, you do too."

And every time my mom and grandma looked up and saw him coming through that back door to do whatever work he was there to do, they would get this mushed-up look on their face, like they were trying to hold their breath for dear life. And we knew Mr. Buck was in the house. The look on their faces told it all. Besides, we didn't have to see him. We could smell him all the way upstairs.

Now my little brother could never keep a secret. From the moment he could talk, he would repeat everything anyone around him said. It didn't matter what the topic was or what was said. If there was anything said by anyone, he would repeat it and tell who said it. And he would do this little rock-steady dance as he talked in that little sing-song voice of his. That's how me and Anthony know how good his secret was. The better the secret, the harder he would dance and the more woo-woos he would drop as he sang.

So one evening my father came home after closing up his shop and told my mom and grandma that Mr. Buck would be over the next day to start on the living room walls. When he said that, my mom and grandma told him they didn't want Mr. Buck in the house anymore.

My father asked them, "Why? What was wrong with Mr. Buck?"

Not knowing my little brother was listening, my mom and grandma started venting about Mr. Buck. They said, "He is nasty. He never cleaned up after himself, making more work for us. His pants are always hanging off his butt, and he stank."

I guess to them that was all the excuse they needed. He stank!

Then they asked him again, "Why do you always have to hire Mr. Buck?"

And my father said, "I always hire Mr. Buck because he's good at his job and I trust him."

My mom said, "Oh, come on, I know you know someone else who can do just as good a job, maybe even better."

My mom and grandma just would not leave it alone. I think they thought they could double-team him into getting their way.

But my father shut it down and told them, "Look, I already called Mr. Buck and talked to him about it. He's hired! So unless you two know of someone I can trust, who could do a better job, won't jack up the price and charge me an arm and a leg, then please let me know."

That shut them up real quick. They didn't say another word about Mr. Buck because they both knew they were housewives. Their domain was a clean house, cooking, the kids, and shopping. (Hey, this was the seventies). Neither one of them knew the first thing about finding and hiring someone to do that kind of work. So they didn't say anything else. They just sucked their teeth, rolled their eyes and necks, and walked away.

So about two hours later, after everyone had cooled down, my grandma and mom tried again to convince, cajole, bribe, and even threaten my father into changing his mind and calling someone else, but with no success.

Mr. Buck showed up at the back door for work, during dinner, of course. He was carrying a ladder and wearing a T-shirt; some dirty work jeans that could stand on their own; his tool belt, with the crack of his butt already showing; and no coat.

So about a day later Mr. Buck was in the living room working. My mom was in the kitchen cleaning up. My grandma was sitting on the couch in the family room watching TV and wrapped up in a blanket because they had the front and back doors wide open in November because of Mr. Buck.

And here comes my big mouth little brother Lee, sliding his way into the living room where Mr. Buck was working. even after we had all been told to stay out of the man's way.

Even though Anthony and I were upstairs doing our homework, we weren't in our rooms. We were sitting at the top of the landing so we could help each other. And from that position, we could hear everything happening downstairs.

We heard Lee ask Mr. Buck what was he doing? Mr. Buck told him he's taking down all the old paneling from the walls. Lee asked him why? Mr. Buck said that he was going to put up some new wallpaper.

And then Lee started doing his little dance and he told Mr. Buck he has a secret.

And Mr. Buck asked, "Well, what's your secret, little man? Tell the news."

And that was all Mr. Buck had to say, because Lee started dancing, twisting, singing, and woo-wooing in that sing-song voice of his and said, "My mommy and my grandma was talking about you."

Mr. Buck said, "Oh really, little man? Well, tell me. What did they say?"

My big head, big-mouth little brother told that man everything he had heard for the last three days. And I mean everything.

Lee told him that our mom and grandma said he stank. Not stink, but stank. That he always showed up at dinnertime. That he was greedy and that he always came over hungry and looking for food. And that he will sit there and eat up all the food like he lives here and bought it or something. That he was nasty and left a mess for (OUR MOM) to clean up. And that they wished he would pull up his pants because they were tired of looking at the crack of his crusty, dirty, unwashed ass and nasty underwear.

And every time Lee stopped to take a breath, Mr. Buck would say, "What else did they say, little man? Tell me the news."

And Lee would start talking and dancing again. He even told Mr. Buck, "Mom and grandma said they had to leave the doors open when you are here because of your smell and that they would rather freeze than smell his sweaty ass. And if they had their way you wouldn't be here at all, because they tried to get my daddy to find someone else to do this job."

And Mr. Buck said, "Oh, really?" By now I think Mr. Buck knew he had gotten just about all the information he could out of Lee. But just to be sure he asked Lee, "Is their anything else?"

And while still dancing and singing, this boy had the nerve to ask Mr. Buck, "Why don't you ever take a bath?"

Mr. Buck asked, "Who says I don't take baths?"

Lee said, "My mom and my grandma said you don't take baths. They said that's why you stink so bad. And you do stink, Mr. Buck. You stink right now."

By the time Lee stopped dancing, Mr. Buck was so mad he just walked out, leaving his ladder and tool box. He didn't say anything to my mom or my grandma. He just walked out the front door. Leaving a mess for mommy to clean up, again.

He went straight over to our father's shop and told him he was sorry but he couldn't finish the job for him. When our father asked him why, he told him everything Lee told him. He said, "I'm sorry but I can't go back to your house knowing how your wife and mother feel about me. And especially now, knowing everything they have said." He just walk out of the shop, still mad, with my father apologizing and promising to find out what was going on and give him a call.

My father finished up at the shop, locked up, and came home right then and there. When he walked in the house, my father was not just mad, he was livid. Anthony and I knew someone was in trouble because of the tension.

At first he wouldn't talk much. I mean, he talked but not like he usually did. His comments and answers were short, like he was holding something back. We could tell he was mad about something.

We were eating dinner and was almost finished when he finally asked my mom and grandma where was Mr. Buck.

They both looked up from the table, looked at each other, and said they didn't know. (Remember, Mr. Buck left out the front door without saying anything to anyone.)

Then my mom said, "We thought he was over at the shop with you."

My father said, "Oh, he stopped by the shop. And he told me how Lee came into the living room dancing and singing and repeated everything you two had been saying about him."

My mom looked over at my little brother and said, "Oh, boy, get up! I am going to whoop your little red butt. I have told you about running your mouth and repeating everything you hear!"

My father told her, "Oh no, you're not gonna whoop him and blame him for repeating the things you and Momma said. You shouldn't have said it. Now I have to figure out what I can say to this man to get him to come back over here and finish this job."

All my mom and grandma could do was sit there with their heads down like two little kids and giving Lee the evil eye.

Now I don't know what my father said or did to get Mr. Buck to come back, but it worked. Mr. Buck came back and went back to work on the living room like nothing ever happened. But that definitely didn't stop them from hiding the food and opening the doors every time he showed up.

The End.

LISA RUNS AWAY

This story is dedicated to my mother,
a strong woman who didn't play no games.

Growing up with my grandma and my cousins on Pine St., I guess we were a little spoiled because we never had to eat food we didn't like.

My uncles and my aunts were always saying, "Y'all need to learn to eat everything on your plates because there are hungry children out there who would be glad to have that food."

And we would tell them, "Well, Grandma said if we don't like it, we don't have to eat it. So you can give those hungry children my peas, my string beans, my squash, and all that other nasty food you are trying to put on our plate."

Or they would say, "Umm, umm, umm, y'all just waste food."

And we would say, "Well, it wouldn't go to waste if you didn't put it on our plate in the first place. Don't put it on our plate, just give it to those hungry kids."

Of course, we all had special things we liked to eat. Mine was pancakes.

When I was about six, after me and my mom moved to West Began, my mom tried to pull rank and change the system. But I was satisfied with the old system, Grandma's system.

So one night for dinner my mom decided to cook fried pork chops for dinner. Okay, that's cool. I like pork chops. Also, mac 'n' cheese. Okay, I like mac 'n' cheese. That's good. And boiled okra. Okra? Really? Boiled okra! Oh hell, no.

So when we all sat down to eat, my mom put my plate in front of me and I looked down at this slimy stuff sliding all over my plate. I looked up at her and said, "Mommy, what is this?"

She said, "What?" Like she didn't know what I was talking about and was trying to play stupid or something.

I said, "This. This slimy stuff. What is it?"

She said, "Oh, it's called okra. Now eat your food."

I looked back down at my plate and said 'I'm not eating that, it's nasty.' And she said 'Yes you are. You see, your grandmother got you spoiled.

Now, I am a very picky eater. If it don't look right or smell right, Lisa won't eat it. And she knows this, so why would she even put something like that on my plate, I don't know. Unless she was looking for a battle.

So I said, "Well, I would have eaten the pork chops and the mac 'n' cheese, but that slime from the okra got all over it and contaminated it. So now I can't eat that either."

And she said, "Well, you might as well eat it because you're not getting up from that table until you do."

So about an hour later, after everybody else finished eating and my mom had finished washing the dishes and cleaning up the kitchen, she pulled out the chair next to me, sat down, and said, "Lisa, you are gonna eat this food, and you're not getting anything else until you do."

When she said that, I thought, *Hey, that's just fine with me because I got some coffee cakes and some banana Now & Laters candy stashed upstairs in my room that I can eat tonight when I go to bed.* And I said with a sigh, because by now I was so tired of talking about this, "Nooo! I. Am. Not. Eating. That! I'm not. You know what grandma said. We don't have to eat food we don't like.

And she said, "How do you know you don't like it? You haven't even tasted it."

I said, "I know I don't like it because it stinks and it's slimy. Look at it! It's sliding all over the plate. I'm not eating that!"

Now during all this I could hear, even though they thought they were whispering, my father and his mother, my grandmother Nora, who lived with us in the next room, laughing, snickering, and making bets on who was gonna win this one. Really! They were laughing and making bets.

And I was thinking, *Why are ya'll in there laughing? Y'all need to come get this woman and put her in check.*

That was when my mom said, "I don't care what your grandma said. In this house I make the rules, and you are gonna do what I tell you to do. Not your grandma."

So I said, "Well, I don't have to live with you. I'm running away. I can go live with my grandma. And I'm gonna tell her that you tried to make me eat your nasty food and the things you said, and she's gonna slap you down like she did before."

When I said that, I saw my mom's face change a little bit. And I thought, *Oh yeah, I got her now. She's gonna stop messing with me.* So my dumbass said it again. "I'm running away, and you just wait until I get to Grandma's house. I'm gonna tell her everything, and she's gonna get you."

But I guess I said that once too often, because after those words left my mouth, all it did was bring her rage to the forefront. Oh, she was mad. My mother's whole face changed. Her eyes turned from light brown to dark brown and squinted all up. Her voice changed, and her face got all red and hot looking.

That was when she grabbed me by my arm, snatched me up from that kitchen chair, and dragged me upstairs, fussing and cussing all the way.

She said, "I'm sick of this shit! Every time I tell you to do something you want to go running to your grandmother! And now you want to run away too? That's fine, come on, I'll help you pack."

When we got upstairs she pulled out my little green suitcase that I always use when we travel and started throwing my clothes in it while saying, "Here, you're gonna need plenty of T-shirts because it's cold outside. And you have to have lots of underwear because you don't ever want the police or anyone else to see you in dirty underwear."

That was back when every potty-trained little girl in the world had those days-of-the-week underwear that we tried our best to keep up with.

Then she shoved my black raggedy Ann doll in my arms and said "Here, make sure you take Ann with you because I'm sick of her shit too." Then she closed my suitcase and said, "Well I think you got everything you need, so let's go."

We went back downstairs to the backdoor, where she put my coat, my shoes, my gloves, scarf and cap on me and said, "Okay, you're all set." and started unlocking the door.

I think she thought I was gonna bust out in tears, sit back down, and eat that nasty food that was still sitting on the table. But, hey I'm a Taurus, and I'm stubborn as hell, you're not gonna make me cry. Or eat that food.

As she started turning the backdoor knob and opening the door I said "Wait, I forgot something." and ran back upstairs. I got the pocketbook my grandma gave me, put my coffee cakes, my banana now & laters, and dumped all the change I had into it. Which was about two 2 dollars in nickles, dimes, and quarters... Hey, to a six 6-year-old, that's a lot of money.

Then I ran back downstairs to the backdoor and said "I'm ready now." rolled my eyes at her, twisted my neck, and walked out the backdoor. Dragging my suitcase (because it was too heavy to lift), my pocketbook and Ann with me.

As I started walking down the driveway I noticed it was really dark outside, and the backlight only went so far before there was a big patch of darkness I had to get through before I could get to the sidewalk and the street lights.

As I was standing there looking at how dark it was and trying to figure out how I could get through it the dogs next door started barking. At what? I didn't know. But I knew it wasn't me because they knew me. So i started backing up, back into the light and sat down on the back step. Trying to think of a way I could get my mom to drive me over to grandma's house in her car.

While I was sitting there, the cold started seeping through my coat. And that's when I heard this scuffling sound in the back yard. It sounded like something was messing around in the truck tires my father had stacked up back there. I looked over to where I thought I heard the sounds coming from and saw a big dark shadow moving around.

I jumped up from that step and started pounding on that back door as hard as I could. Because I just knew I saw a monster out there and he was coming for me.

When my mom finally opened the door, this women had the nerve to say "What are you doing here? You and Ann don't live here anymore." and I said "we're not moving back in here (like I had been gone for years or something.) We're just gonna stay here until morning because there is a big monster out here messing with the tires. "My mom stuck her head out the door, looked around real quick, and said "I don't see nothing, but okay. I will let you stay here tonight, but you and Ann have to leave in the morning. Now take off your stuff and take your suitcase back upstairs to your room."

After I did that. I came back downstairs to take a hot bath and get ready for bed. And while the bathwater was running, my grandma Nora asked "if I was hungry? And did I want her to make me a plate?" looking at my mom I said, "Yes, but I don't want any of that slimy okra on my plate." As I followed her into the kitchen and watched her make my plate, just in case.

While I was eating my food, I told my father "You need to get your gun, go outside and kill that monster so he won't bother us when me and Ann leave tomorrow," and he said "Don't worry, the monster won't be there when you leave because they only come out at night."

That's when my grandma Nora started laughing again and told my father "I want my money."

I swear this family is crazy. As long as you don't die, it becomes a joke.

BAPTIZED

This story is dedicated to my sister/cousin Danai, our warrior. She ain't afraid of nothing.

Okay, I remember one year my grandmother joined a church right around the corner from her house, on the corner of Ridge Avenue. After joining this church she signed us girls up for Bible study, and every Sunday she would take us to church with her. We would go downstairs to Bible study, and after it was over, we would go upstairs and join her for the rest of the church service.

So one year Grandma came to us and said we were now old enough to be baptized into her church. When she told us about it, we didn't think anything of it. But that was because we had never seen anyone baptized before. And with the way she described it, it was like it was gonna be this special day for us, that it would gain us favor in God's eye, and it only took a little dunk in a pool of blessed water.

When she said this, I assumed this pool would be like a little kiddie's wading pool and that it might even be fun. So when this special day of ours came along, it was kinda chilly, and when we got to the church, the doors weren't open yet. While we waited, Grandma started talking to some of the other ladies there. The other children and I were just standing around, bored as hell. We couldn't play because we didn't want to get our clothes dirty, and we all know kids do not listen in or comment on grown folks' conversations—not if you want to keep all of your teeth.

So while we waited, we asked Grandma if we could run over to the candy store and get some stuff before the service starts.

She said, "Yes, but hurry up because they will be opening the doors soon."

So we ran off, trying to get to the store as fast as we could with those Sunday shoes hurting our feet and click-clacking all the way.

When we got there we spent every dime we had on Now & Laters, Blow Pops, and coffee cakes. We even combined our last pennies together to get Big Bol bubble gums and divided them evenly between us. By the time we got back to the church, the doors were open and everyone was already inside sitting down. So we found our grandmother and scuttled our way down the pews, while trying not to step on anyone's toes, and sat down. And as soon as our butts hit those seats, we started talking, digging into our bags, and stuffing our faces, trying not to make too much noise or talk to loud because we didn't want Grandma to have to tell us to be quiet too many times because she will pinch our legs.

I don't know how long that service lasted because it seemed like it took forever. But I do know by the end of it, my sister/cousin Liz, the baby, fell asleep in Grandma's lap. I fell asleep on Danai's shoulder. And Danai was trying to stay awake by reading Grandma's Bible.

So, finally, the service was over and Grandma took us in the back to take off our clothes and change into these long robes. While changing, Liz, Danai, and I were talking about who was gonna go first. And it kinda turned into an argument because Danai as the oldest was always trying to take control and tell us what to do.

So, finally, Grandma stepped in and told us, "Danai is the oldest. And as the oldest, she is going to go first." Then next would be me and then Liz. And as long as we do everything the preacher says, it will be over in no time.

That's when I started wondering what she was talking about. I mean, I thought all we had to do was stand in a wading pool of holy water, just full enough to get our feet wet while the preacher prays and makes a cross on our foreheads with his thumb dipped in holy water and that was it, right? So what was she talking about "all we had to do was do what the preacher tell us and it will be over before we know it"? What did he have to do besides pray and mark our foreheads?

I found out real quick there was more to it than that. A whole lot more.

So after we were finished changing, we went back to the front of the church and lined up with the other children. As the other children went up on the stage, that's when I saw it wasn't just a wading pool to cover your feet. They were stepping down into a deep pool of water and was being dunked down into it by the preacher. As we got closer, I could hear the children that had went before us talking about "how the water was cold" and that "the preacher was too rough when dunking them and he didn't tell them to hold their breath."

After hearing all this, I told Grandma I didn't want to do it.

She told me, "Oh, don't worry. There was nothing to it. All big girls have to be baptized. Just watch Danai."

So that's what I did. I watched Danai because I knew I was next. And when Danai got up there, I saw she had to walk down into this pool of water that came all the way up to her waist. The preacher put one hand over her mouth, grabbed her by the back of her head with the other hand, said a few words, and then dunked her down in the water while still preaching. He held her down under the water so long she started fighting. Even though she was fighting, he still held her under until he finished his prayer. And when he finally let her up, she was gasping for air and trying to breathe.

When I saw that, I turned around and took off running. I heard my grandma and my baby sister/cousin Liz calling my name, but I didn't think twice. I was gone, leaving Liz the next in line on her own. I was running for my life. And I didn't stop until I hit the front door of my house on West Began.

A few minutes later my grandma called to see if I had gotten home okay and to let my mom know she was coming by to get the church's robe that I still had on and to deliver the clothes that I left behind.

And to this day I have not been baptized.

The End.

BUTCH THE GANGSTER

This story is dedicated to my dog, Butch,
a little thirty-pound gangster.

Growing up in Red Bank we have always had dogs. We are a dog family. When I was two years old, we moved to West Began place and we already had Sheba. She was my older brother, Anthony's dog. A big sheepdog that used to lie on me, grab me by my shirt sleeve, and drag me around the house with her like I was her puppy. She died when I was ten.

After she died, my father brought home a mix-breed Ridgeback dog named Trey. He used to run from the back door, through the house, up the stairs, through the bedrooms, back down the stairs, to the back door, and back again. He would only stop long enough to wolf down his food real quick and drink some water, and then he would start the running all over again until he passed out for the night. (I think he was on drugs.) He would do this every day until my mom got tired of him wrecking the house by knocking over and breaking things during his all-day sprint throughout the house. And she said he had to go. That took about two days.

Then we got a black Newfoundland puppy I named Duke. We had him about six months before he got sick and died. Then we got the cutest little collie mix puppy that I named Butch. He was nothing but a little ball of fur with eyes. Now, at this time in my life I didn't know dogs had attitudes. I knew they get mad at you. I knew they got jealous. I even knew they held grudges. But I didn't know they got attitudes. I didn't find this out until we got Butch. And we learned real quick that this little boy was crazy and he had no fear in his heart. He would try to fight anything—human or animal. It didn't matter how big. He didn't care. I called it the Napoleon complex. His mind told him he was bigger and stronger then he really was.

I thought that drugged-out mix-breed Ridgeback that ran through the house like a bat out of hell until he passed out was off. But Butch was all- out crazy. He was a very smart and obedient dog, he never ran off, he pretty much house trained himself, he checked the house every night to make sure everyone was in their beds before he went to sleep, and he was very protective. But with all that he was still crazy.

We use to come to North Carolina for two weeks every summer for vacation before we actually moved here, and we would always bring Butch with us. He went everywhere we went—until he got himself in trouble, that is.

One day all the kids were all sitting outside on our porch in North Carolina. We were in the south, in the summer, and it was way too hot to do anything else. Then we saw Butch chasing and jumping back from something in the yard, like he was playing with it. But we really couldn't see what it was. So we just started calling him to come back up on the porch with us, but he wouldn't come. And this was not like Butch. He usually always listened and obeyed us, so whatever he was messing with had his full attention and was very interesting to him. So my brother Anthony stood up and went down a couple of the porch steps so he could see what Butch had, and that was when Anthony saw it. It was a poisonous black snake.

When Anthony told us that, everyone started yelling and screaming for Butch to come to us because black snakes are deadly. I ran in the house to get the adults and tell them that Butch found a black snake in the yard and was messing with it. They came running out of the house and went to the outdoor closet where they kept the yard tools and got shovels and a pickax. Meantime, we were still trying to get Butch to come away from it. But Butch was so into messing with this snake that he never even looked up.

They had to kill this snake without hitting Butch because he still wouldn't leave it alone. He just kept biting and snapping at it. After the men killed it, Butch finally got his chance to get a bite in, shake it, and slam it to the ground with a few barks and growls thrown in. Then he came prancing back to us with a smile on his face, his tongue hanging out like he was the killer of all dog killers looking for his props. I mean, really, he was so proud of himself. He actually thought he did something.

After Butch came back to the porch, he flopped down in front of us like he was the king of the house. My father went and got some gas and poured it on the snake, and eight eggs popped out. So not only was this snake deadly poisonous, it was also a female. A pregnant female with eight eggs that also had to be killed.

After that day Butch was no longer allowed to go with us to North Carolina. I realized he was very fascinated with this snake because he had never seen one before. But what got him in trouble is the fact that he wouldn't listen to us. He wouldn't come to us when called, and that was a no-no. So he brought this on himself.

So my mom decided she would leave Butch with my aunt whenever we go to North Carolina. That kind of pissed me off because Butch was always treated like he was another brother. And I didn't like going to North Carolina anyway. It was too damn hot. I felt like if Butch could stay home with my aunt, why can't I? So I asked my mom if I could stay home too, and of course she said no!

Butch was mad because he wanted to go, and I was mad because I didn't want to go. Ain't that some shit. Now, after we left him with my aunt the first time, we thought everything was fine. We didn't receive any phone calls saying he ran away or was missing or anything, so we thought everything was cool. So as soon as we hit

Red Bank, we went over to my aunt's house to pick him up and he wouldn't get in the car. I couldn't believe it. Usually, Butch couldn't wait for the car door to open so he could claim his seat, which was always my lap. But this time he wouldn't get in the car. He walked home, and he got there before us.

When we got home and finally got in the house after an eight-hour drive from North Carolina, Butch was so mad he wouldn't even come to us. Oh, we called his name and we reached out to pet and touch him, but he would step around us, out of reach, as if to say, "Don't touch me, you traitor."

I mean, really. This from a dog. I mean, he did know he was a dog, right? And he would act like this every day until he got his chance to get us back for leaving him. Oh, he was slick with it. He would get us to follow him into the living room where he knew my mom and grandma Nora couldn't see him.

He would get us to follow him into the living room where he knew my mom and grandmother couldn't see him. Then he would play with us and wrestle with us like everything was cool—until he got us down on the floor. Then he would go in for the attack. He would drag me around on that living room carpet by my hair until I had rug burns and my hair was sticking up all over my head full of dog slob.

Then he would go after my little brothers, Lee and Keith. He would get Lee by his shirt and sling him around the living room until he screamed for Mommy. Lee's arms and stomach would be all scratched up.

Then my baby brother Keith was next. He would get Keith by his butt and just shake him like he was one of his rag toys or an old sock or something. Keith's butt would be all bruised up like he had just gotten a whopping. Well, I guess he did, huh?

But he wouldn't do this to our older brother Anthony, our parents, or our grandmother. Just me and my two younger brothers. Oh, we would scream and cry for Mommy. But that didn't mean anything because Butch wouldn't let us out of that living room until he was done.

When we called our mother for help, she would say, "Oh no, don't call me! If you are stupid enough to follow him into that living room where you know I can't see you and to play with him when you know he's still mad and you get beat up, do not call me, just come on in here with the Alcohol, the Cotton Balls, and the Band-Aids so I can patch your dumb ass up."

Even though Butch wouldn't touch our parents, our older brother Anthony, or our grandmother, he would still most definitely let us know how he felt about things. Then after he got his much-needed revenge he would be fine. Like nothing ever happened.

My brothers Lee and Keith and I would be walking around all patched up and sore like we had just walked through a war zone. And Butch would be walking around all happy, tongue hanging out, smiling and everything. The perfect little family pet—until the next time we left him with my aunt and went to North Carolina without him.

God, I loved that dog.

The End.

THE MEANING
OF HORSEPOWER

This story is dedicated to my older brother, Anthony.
He loved me, protected me, advised me, was the holder of all my secrets, and made sure I was always treated like the queen I am.
RIP, Anthony. You are truly missed.

I know y'all are going to laugh at me and say I was a stupid little girl, but I don't care.

I don't remember how old I was, but I remember one summer my father bought my mom her first car for her birthday. A brown mustang.

And my big brother Anthony was outside in the driveway one afternoon checking out the new car. He had the hood up, looking at the engine, like he knew what he was doing.

So me and my nosey self went outside and asked Anthony 'What are you doing?'

He said, "Nothing," then told me to leave him alone and to mind my own business.

But I just kept standing there asking him stupid questions about anything and everything.

By now I knew I was getting on his nerves, but I didn't care because secretly that was my intention from the beginning. That was the main reason why I went out there.

So finally I asked him "What makes a car run?"

He told me that this car ran on horsepower and that not all cars did, but this car ran on horsepower.

So I asked him, "What is horsepower?"

Anthony said, "You are so stupid. You don't know what horsepower means?"

I said, "I'm not stupid, but no, I don't know what horsepower means. What is it?"

He said, "Horsepower meant that the car had little tiny horses in it. And that when you turned the key in the ignition, it will shock the little horses into running. And that's what made this car run. That's why it was called a Ford Mustang. Mustangs are a breed of horse."

So I asked Anthony, "How many little horses are in there?"

And he said, "From what the car book says, this car has about two hundred."

When he said that, I thought, *Wow! Two hundred! That's a lot of horses.*

So I switched up my voice to that sweet little girl's voice I always used on my father when I wanted something. I mean, it always worked on my father, why wouldn't it work on Anthony. He is my older brother. Isn't it their job to take care of their little sister?

So I asked him in that voice so nice and so sweet most people would have walked away with a cavity. "Anthony, can I have one of those little horsies in there?"

And he said, "No!"

No? I couldn't believe it. I knew I had to be hearing wrong. He didn't say that. So I said, "What? What did you say?"

And he said that word again, "No."

I couldn't believe it. No! With me being the only girl in the house with three brothers, I was spoiled rotten. I didn't ask for much. I didn't have to. But when I did asked for something, I got it. And right now I wanted one of those little horsies.

So I ran into the house, and I asked my mom (this shows just how much parents listen to their kids' nonsense), "Mommy, can I have one of the little horsies out of your new car?"

And she said, "Sure, if you can find one."

So, happy as hell I ran upstairs to my bedroom, got my fishbowl, ran back downstairs to the bathroom, and flushed my goldfish Oliver down the toilet. I washed out Oliver's fishbowl real quick, ran back outside and put some grass from the yard in the bottom of it.

Then I skipped my happy ass back over to where Anthony was (still messing around with Mommy's car) with this little grin on my face and said (like the spoiled little girl I was), "Anthony, Mommy said I can have one of the little horsies from her car, so you need to reach in there, get me one out, and put it in my bowl. Oh, and make sure it's a pregnant girl horse, so when she has the baby, I will have two."

And again he said, "No!"

So now, after a lot of arguing with him, I was mad. And no matter what I said he still wouldn't get me my little horse.

So I went back into the house and waited until our father came home after closing up the shop that night, thinking, *Oh yeah, I'm gonna get my little pregnant horse and I'm gonna get Anthony in trouble because he didn't just get it when I told him to.* Ohhhh, this was gonna be gooood.

So I waited for our father to get home after closing the shop that night. And I had the tears and the story all set to go as soon as he walked through that back door. I was thinking, *Yeah, I'm gonna get my little horse now.*

So as soon as our father walked through that door I was on him, with the tears going and everything. When he saw me crying and coming toward him, he said, "Lisa, what's wrong with you?"

That was all the hint I needed to start my story. I ran up to him and told him, "Mommy said I could have one of the little horses in her car, and Anthony was being mean because he wouldn't get it for me."

My father looked at me and asked, "What in the world are you talking about?"

So after I explained everything to him from the beginning, I was thinking, *Yeah, Anthony, you're in trouble now.*

But instead, my father, my mother, and my grandmother (who lived with us) looked at me and started laughing even though I was still crying. Hey, it took a lot for me to get those fake tears going, okay? I'm not a professional at this. I usually don't have to work this hard to get something I want. So I was gonna work those tears for all they were worth. And they had the nerve to be laughing at me.

And that was when my father told me, "There are no little horses in that car or any other." He said that he couldn't believe I would be so gullible as to believe that story—even if it was Anthony that told it to me.

I told him, "But I asked Mommy and she said I could have one if I could find it."

He asked me, "Well, did you find it?"

When I said no, he said, "That's because you can't find what doesn't exist."

And when I told him how I flushed my goldfish Oliver down the toilet so I could put the horse in the bowl, he said, "It's okay, Oliver is fine and is living with his family and friends in the drain."

The next day when I came home from my cousin's house, I had two new goldfish in the bowl on my desk and a new stuffed horse sitting on my bed. The fish were from my brother Anthony (RIP) and the horse was from my mom.

The End.

DEALING
WITH THE DEVIL

I have got to dedicate this story to my cousin J.M. (you know who you are) Someone who has been through a lot in life and has still found the courage in him to fight through that demon from childhood and become a success. He kicked it in the ass and won.

Growing up on(West Began St.), there was this plot of grassy land right next to the bar with a metal pipe around it. I don't know if there was once a building there that was connected to the bar or what. But it was diagonally across the street from my father's tire shop. And everyone at the shop could see everything we did over there. I was just told to stay on my side of the street. But I was never told why. I was just to stay on my side of the street and not to walk or play over there.

But of course, I just couldn't do as I was told. And telling me to do something without an explanation was just like telling me to do it. All it did was make me want to do just that... besides, every spring the grass grew so long, pretty, and green over there. And like most girls, I just couldn't resist. I knew something wasn't right about that spot. I could feel it. My instincts and my family told me to stay away. And even though my stomach would clench up, and I would start sweating in fear. For some reason, I still just could not stay away. I kept going over there anyway, ignoring my instincts and feelings. And something bad happened every time. Not from my parents, but from others.

Like, one day me and my cousin Margie, who lived across the street were over there using the metal pipe to flip over, and I hit the back of my head on the ground so hard I was bleeding.

Another time I was walking home from school on that side of the street. And this girl named Connie just kept messing with me. She just kept pushing me in my back and pulling my hair.

Now, I did not want to fight this girl. I really didn't. I had just got out of the hospital the weekend before. After having another sickle cell crisis and I wasn't feeling all that good yet. I was still kind of soar. And I just wanted to go home and do my homework in peace. But this girl just would not stop. And as a Taurus from Red Bank, ya'll know I was only going to let this girl go so far before I turn around and clock her. And that's exactly what happened.

Connie pushed me one too many times. And when I fell, I ripped my favorite shirt. When I saw that, I lost it. I jumped up, turned around and started swinging. She fell over the pipe and I started kicking her. Okay...maybe I shouldn't have kicked her. But hey, maybe she should've left me alone. The next thing I know, my father had snatched me up and was carrying me home over his shoulder.

Okay, so one day I was walking past the lot on my way to a friend's house. And I found a $10. Ten dollar bill laying there on the sidewalk, I picked it up and put it in my pocket. I mean why not it was sitting there wide open for anyone to see it, in broad daylight. But anyway, Back to the story.

Then I saw a white envelope lying on the grass. I walked over and picked it up. And there was $200. Two Hundred Dollars in it. No name. No nothing. Just the money. How come no one else saw it and picked it up before me? I don't know.

I stuck the whole envelope in my other pocket and ran back home to show my mom all this money I had just found. (Big mistake... because I never saw a dime of that money ever again. I should have just kept my mouth shut, hid the money, and went on a shopping spree at Freddie's candy store like I started too.

After leaving the money with my mom, I went back over there to see what else I could find. (I had forgotten all about going over to my friend's house) and while looking around this man named Mack came up behind me and asked me my name.

Of course, I ignored him. At first, I thought maybe he was looking for that money I had found. Maybe it was his. But he never asked about the money. He just asked me my name. You know we are all taught not to speak to strangers. So, I turned around to head back across the street, and as I turned away from him to go home he grabbed me by my wrist and said "why are you being rude? Don't you know it's rude not to answer grown folks when they are speaking to you? Where're your manners? I know your parents taught you better than that." Then he said, "Now I'm gonna ask you again... What's your name?" During all this I never did answer his question, I was too busy trying my hardest to pull away while yelling "get off me!!! Let me go!!!" But it was like being in the twilight zone. Because even though I was yelling for this man to let me go, nobody came. It's like no one could hear me. I'm kicking at his legs and knees, scratching and clawing the hand holding me, and he still wouldn't let go.

Then he said "Fine, you don't have to tell me your name. I already know it, 'Lisa'. But someone needs to teach you some manners." and he started laughing. Then he said "I've been watching you for a while. I like you. You're a pretty little thing. I'm not trying to hurt you. I just want to be friends." During all this I'm still yelling, pulling and fighting as hard as I could. But he still wouldn't let go.

Then while still laughing he said "I wish I had parked my car closer. But I didn't think I would see you today. You and I are gonna be friends. Yes, we are gonna be good friends. But first, you need to be trained. I've got to teach you some manners." And that scared me so bad. Especially when he said "you can stop all this fighting and yelling. No one is paying any attention to us." Then still laughing he said "you only weigh about what? 70 pound? I know you don't think you can hurt me or do anything to stop me. Do you?"

And what scared me the most about what he said is that it was true. There was really nothing I could do to stop him from dragging me to his car and taking me away and doing whatever he wanted to do to me. Especially since it seemed no one heard me yelling or saw me fighting him.

Then I remembered I had a little box cutter my older brother Anthony gave me in my back pocket. And while he was still talking and laughing I pulled out that box cutter and cut him across the back of the hand that was holding my wrist. When I did that he let go of me, I fell back on my butt, while he jumped back and screamed "Ohww!!! You little bitch!!" That's when I noticed my uncle and two other men coming across the street. They were yelling at Mack as they came "Hey!! What are you doing?!!" and Mack said "Oh hi. How are you doing?" and my uncle said, "I asked you a question. What the hell are you doing?" and Mack said "Nothing. I was just talking to this girl. You know how disrespectful these kids are these days? And damn, she cut me on my hand...look at this...I really should take my belt off and whoop her butt for this."

I guess Mack didn't know me like he said he did.(other than my name) or he would have known this was my uncle and 2 Two of his friends. But he found out real quick.

By the time I got up off the ground my uncle and his two friends were there surrounding him. My uncle grabbed Mack by his shirt collar, looked at me and told me to go home. As I started running home, I heard one of my uncle's friends say, "We were watching everything from across the street. It didn't look like you were talking to her. It looked like you had her by the arm and wouldn't let her go." Then my uncle said, "That one is mine's. Why were you talking to her anyway?"

As I crossed the street I heard Mack say "I didn't know she was yours, I was just trying to talk to her, that's all." and I stopped at my father's tire shop and told my father and the men there what happened and they all ran across the street too. And my older brother who was working at the shop that day told me to go to the house and tell my mom and grandmother what happened. And that's what I did.

Thank god for my brother Anthony and that box cutter. Because without it I never would've been able to get away from Mack on my own. After this, my brother kept me supplied in knives every year.

I don't know what my father, my uncle and those men said or did to Mack that day, but I know the police were never called. And I never saw Mack again.

Years later, I heard he was a known child molester and rapist. And that he has said "the younger the better. Boy or girl. Because he always wants to be their first. He likes to hear them cry, scream and fight in pain."

And to think, these were his plans for me...

The End.

With this story, I just have to say something.

Adults have got to stop telling children "to always obey adults" and "what goes on in this house stays in this house."

We children of the '50s, '60s, '70s and probably the '80s, have been told that at one time or another all through childhood.

And those are two very dangerous rules to make your children follow. Because with those words you are setting your children up for molestation, rape, and abuse.

Because everyone has a predator in the house. A friend or family member that is a child molester, an abuser, a pedophile or a rapist.

We all know one. And we all have one. Whether we want to believe it or not. You know that family friend, relative or family member the adults are always whispering and pointing about. The uncle, aunt or cousin you are never allowed to go anywhere with, or even be alone with without an adult always coming up and asking "what are you two talking about?" What did he or she ask you?" Because oh yes, they can be women too...

And don't think just because this person is a good or best friend of your parents. Or a person the adults will swear to the grave are good people and will never do something like that. Those are the ones that will.

No child is safe...

And to give our children these rules is setting them up to be victims. And you're giving the abuser, molester, pedophile all the confidence he or she needs to believe they won't get caught. Why??? Because you have already trained your children to keep secrets from you and everybody else. You have already done the predator's work for them.

And this has got to be stopped.

OH, THE THINGS
YOU HAVE DONE

This story is dedicated to my brother/ cousin, the family mechanic
No toy was safe.

I have a lot of family that I grew up with in Red Bank. But being the only girl in my house was lonely. So I spent as much time as I could at my Aunt's house with my brother and sister cousins. Because over there I had two of each to play with, two sister/cousins and 2 two brother/cousins. I was there so much, I practically lived there.

Now that I have laid all that out for you, here we go......

I remember one year me and my sister/ cousins Danai and Liz got dolls and doll strollers for Christmas. But, my brother/cousin Bear was always making things out of our toys. So we learned real quick we had to hide all the toys we really liked and wanted to keep, just so he wouldn't take them and twist them up into something for himself.

So, that spring when Danai, Liz, and I were finally able to pull our dolls and stroller's out of hiding and play with them outside with the other little girls on the street, it was great, we had so much fun we had to be called in for dinner.

We were only able to play with those strollers once or twice that spring, when one day we went to pull them out of hiding and the wheels were gone.

So, of course because of his history the first thing we did was to go looking for Bear. And we asked him straight up "where are the wheels to our dolls strollers?" and Bear looked at us, and had the nerve to say "What doll strollers?" Oh, that made me so mad. I couldn't believe he said that. Really? "What doll strollers?" When he said that he didn't just make me mad, he made Danai and Liz mad too. We were already mad when we noticed the wheels gone, but this took us all the way there.

So, Danai being the oldest and with more authority took over and did all the talking. With her face all scrunched up, she said "Bear, don't play with me. You know exactly what doll strollers. Our doll strollers. Where are the wheels to our doll strollers?" and Bear had the nerve to look us in the face and say "I don't know what you're talking about" and then swore to us he didn't take them. Lying! Just lying!

But of course he would say that, he was surrounded by three mad girls. And we had already talked about it and decided we were going to jump him and beat him up if he had our strollers wheels. But he swore he didn't have them, and Danai said we couldn't just beat him up right now because we didn't catch him with them. At that moment she was playing attorney for the accused.

So, one Saturday a few weeks later the police showed up at the door with bear and a go cart. A go cart with wheels that looked so familiar. Bear had took the wheels off of our doll stroller's and used them and an old car battery he found at the dump to make this go cart. And the police clocked him doing 30 mph up and down West Began St. My street. Just speeding in his illegal go-cart.

The cops pulled him over, took him downtown to the police station and had him down there for hours, talking to him and feeding him McDonald's. While questioning him about how he made it, and who helped him? Because they just couldn't believe this kid made a running co-cart by himself. He was only about ten at the time.

While they were talking to him someone called my father and my uncle to come downtown and pick him up from the station. But after my father picked up my uncle, they talked in the car and decided to teach Bear a lesson. So, when they got to the station my father and uncle told the officers they had a plan to teach Bear a lesson so this won't happen again. They told the officers to tell him that he was being arrested for driving an illegal car without a license, tags or registration and for possession of stolen property (the wheels from our dolls strollers). And that his uncles were only there to say good bye. Because he was on his way to juvie and he will never see home again. And that's what my father and uncle did. They walked into the room and told Bear good bye and then they left. My father and uncle just walked out leaving Bear there, and went back home.

After my father and uncle left, the officer's packed up Bear and his go-cart, loaded them in the car, and told him they were going to drop him off at the jail with the big boys. But first they were going to take him by his house so he can say good bye to his mother and family.

So, by the time they showed up at the front door with him and his go cart, Bear was a crying, boo hooing, blubbering, snotty nose mess, who really believed he would never see us again...

Even though it was funny, at that moment we felt so sorry for him. But that Sunday morning Danai, Liz and I, got up early, snuck into Bear's room while he was still asleep, and jumped him for stealing the wheels off of our dolls strollers and lying about it... After that our toys and strollers were safe and Bear never used our things again. And he definitely never made another go-cart. He just made other things that got him in just as much trouble.

The End.